★ ★ ★ ★ ★ ★ ★ ★ ★ ★ ★ ★ ★ ★ ★ ★ ★ ★ ★ ★ ★ ★ ★ ★ ★ ★ ★

WAR HEROES OF AMERICA

# John Paul Jones

## NAVAL HERO

MATTHEW G. GRANT

Illustrated by John Keely

GALLERY OF GREAT AMERICANS SERIES

★ ★ ★ ★ ★ ★ ★ ★ ★ ★ ★ ★ ★ ★ ★ ★ ★ ★ ★ ★ ★ ★ ★ ★ ★ ★ ★

# John Paul Jones

## NAVAL HERO

Library of Congress Number:   73-18212      ISBN:   0-87191-300-3

Published by Creative Education, Mankato, Minnesota 56001
Distributed by Childrens Press, 1224 West Van Buren Street, Chicago, Illinois 60607

**Library of Congress Cataloging in Publication Data**
Grant, Matthew G.
    John Paul Jones — naval hero.
    (His Gallery of Great Americans series. War heroes of America)
    SUMMARY: A brief biography of John Paul Jones stressing his naval career.
    1. Jones, John Paul, 1747-1792 — Juvenile literature. (1. Jones, John Paul, 1747-1792.
2. United States — History — Revolution — Biography)  I. Keely, John, illus.   II. Title.
E207.J7G73      973.3'5'0924 (B) (92)      73-18212
ISBN 0-87191-300-3

# CONTENTS

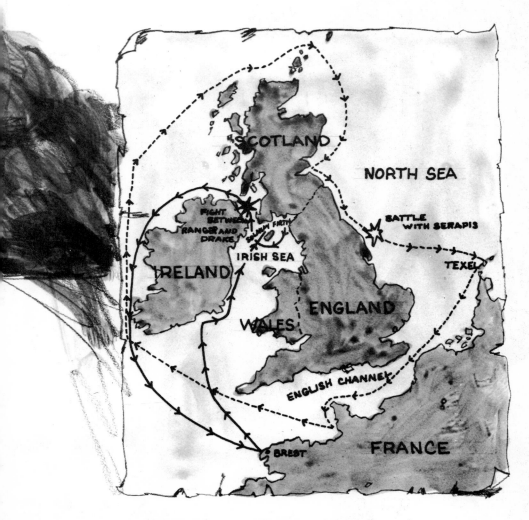

NORTH SEA

SCOTLAND

FIGHT
BETWEEN
RANGER AND
DRAKE

SOLWAY FIRTH

BATTLE
WITH SERAPIS

IRELAND

IRISH SEA

TEXEL

ENGLAND

WALES

ENGLISH CHANNEL

BREST

FRANCE

←‹← CRUISE OF THE RANGER 1778

·‹·‹·‹· CRUISE OF THE BON HOMME RICHARD 1779

## A HOT-TEMPERED SAILOR

In 1761, a gardener's son named John Paul, Jr., left his home in Arbigland, Scotland. He was 13 years old. It was time for him to learn a trade, and he wanted to become a sailor.

For three years, he was an apprentice seaman on a brig. He sailed between Scotland, the West Indies, and Virginia in the American colonies. Then John wanted to learn the duties of a ship's officer. But he was so young that the only berths open to him were on slave ships. His ambition overcame his conscience and he served as mate on ''blackbirders'' for the next two years.

In 1768, he quit his job on a slave ship and sailed home to Scotland as a passenger. While at sea, the ship's captain and mate died of a fever. It was up to John to get the vessel safely to port. He did this so well that the ship's owners made him a captain at the age of 21.

Captain John Paul became known as an excellent — if rather overbearing — merchant seaman.

His youth and his short stature, five feet six inches, put him at a disadvantage when dealing with tough sailors. So he built up self-confidence by wearing elegant clothes and carrying a sword. If a sailor was slow to obey, Captain Paul had him flogged.

One man who was whipped later took sick of a fever and died. Charges were brought

11

against John Paul, but the courts later cleared him completely.

John Paul's temper finally ruined his civilian career. In 1773, his ship anchored at the West Indies island of Tobago. The crew wanted money, but Paul refused to give it to them. One ringleader from among the crew tried to strike the captain with a club.

Overcome with fury, Paul killed the man with his sword. In the uproar that followed, Paul was forced to flee from the island and change his name.

## IN THE CONTINENTAL NAVY

He became ''John Paul Jones'' and made his way to America. There the Revolutionary War was just breaking out. John Paul Jones enlisted in the brand-new Continental Navy as a lieutenant.

In Spring, 1776, the Navy consisted of eleven vessels of various sizes. Eight of them went off to raid the Bahama Islands. Lt. Jones served on the flagship, Alfred. Later that year he got his own command, the small but fast sloop Providence.

Almost at once, he proved himself to

be a daring seafighter. He captured seven British ships as prizes-of-war and successfully dodged a warship's guns.

Jones became a hero overnight. He was given command of the Alfred. Sailing up toward Canada, he captured more prizes and did battle with British frigates.

When he returned to port, he expected to be promoted. Unfortunately, he had made many enemies because of his hot temper and criticism of other officers. Even worse, he was not American-born. Congress regarded him as a "foreigner." He had to go back to the Providence.

## BONHOMME RICHARD

In 1777, Jones was sent to France to take delivery of a new ship. While in Paris, he became the friend of Benjamin Franklin, the statesman-scientist, author of Poor Richard's Almanac.

Franklin helped persuade France to declare war on Britain. When this happened, in 1778, Jones was able to use French ports as a base for raiding England.

He took the warship Ranger to the British west coast, not far from his birthplace, and attacked the town of Whitehaven. Then, in a spectacular battle, he captured a British warship, H.M.S. Drake. People in England wrote songs about the daring Yankee raider.

The next year, Jones was given command of a ship twice as big as the Ranger. He named his vessel Bonhomme Richard (Goodfellow Richard), in honor of Franklin's almanac.

Bonhomme Richard and four other American vessels went raiding around Ireland and Scotland, capturing many prize ships on the way. Then, on September 23, 1779, Captain Jones spotted a convoy of 41 British merchant ships, guarded by two men-of-war.

The powerful British frigate H.M.S. Serapis came after the Richard. John Paul Jones was in a desperate position. His ship was old and slow and out-gunned. He knew his only chance lay in grappling Serapis and boarding her.

Cannons blazing, the two ships drifted together. The wind was nearly dead calm. The old Richard took a fearful pounding and many guns were knocked out of action.

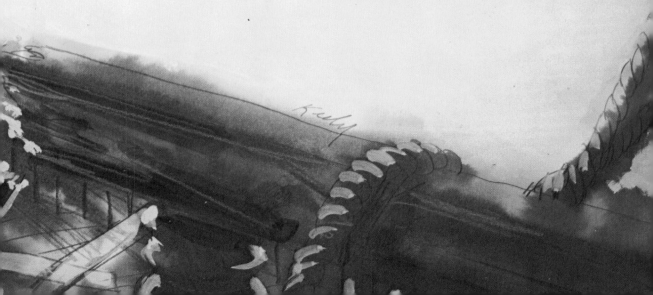

The British captain tried to sail around the Richard. Jones's ship rammed the Britisher's stern.

The English captain called out, asking if Jones was ready to surrender.

John Paul Jones shouted: "I have not yet begun to fight!"

For two more hours the ships clung together, tied by grappling cables. Richard began to sink.

But French musketeers aboard the Richard kept on picking off British gunners. A brave Yankee sailor crawled out on a mast and dropped grenades into the hold of Serapis,

exploding her powder. Jones, with only three cannons left, managed to topple the mainmast of Serapis. It was enough. The British ship surrendered. Jones sailed the captured Serapis back to France. The gallant Bonhomme Richard sank two days after the great battle.

## SEAMAN'S SUNSET

In 1780, Franklin sent John Paul Jones to America with a cargo of badly needed supplies. The French nobility had made a great fuss over the heroic captain, and he was very reluctant to leave Paris.

Back in Philadelphia, Jones was at first treated as a hero. But then his old habit of criticizing others made him seem a nuisance and a bore. Congress refused to make him an admiral. When the war ended, the Navy was abolished. Jones protested in vain that

America still needed its Navy in order to survive as a nation. He begged Congress to rebuild the Navy and set up an academy to train officers. But no one listened—then.

In 1787, John Paul Jones left America and went to live in Paris, where he felt people were friendly to his ideas. He did not know what to do with himself. Empress Catherine of Russia offered him the post of rear admiral, and for one year he commanded a squadron of ships in the Black Sea. He helped the Russians defeat the Turks in the Second Battle of Liman. But the Russians did not give him the glory he wanted.

He resigned from the Russian Navy and went back to Paris. He died there, of pneumonia, in 1792.

America finally came to appreciate the deeds and beliefs of John Paul Jones. President Theodore Roosevelt sent vessels of the U.S. Navy to France in 1905, to bring his body back home. The naval hero of the American Revolution was reburied in the chapel of the Naval Academy at Annapolis.

# GALLERY OF GREAT AMERICANS SERIES

### INDIANS OF AMERICA
GERONIMO
CRAZY HORSE
CHIEF JOSEPH
PONTIAC
SQUANTO
OSCEOLA

### EXPLORERS OF AMERICA
COLUMBUS
LEIF ERICSON
DeSOTO
LEWIS AND CLARK
CHAMPLAIN
CORONADO

### FRONTIERSMEN OF AMERICA
DANIEL BOONE
BUFFALO BILL
JIM BRIDGER
FRANCIS MARION
DAVY CROCKETT
KIT CARSON

### WAR HEROES OF AMERICA
JOHN PAUL JONES
PAUL REVERE
ROBERT E. LEE
ULYSSES S. GRANT
SAM HOUSTON
LAFAYETTE

### WOMEN OF AMERICA
CLARA BARTON
JANE ADDAMS
ELIZABETH BLACKWELL
HARRIET TUBMAN
SUSAN B. ANTHONY
DOLLEY MADISON